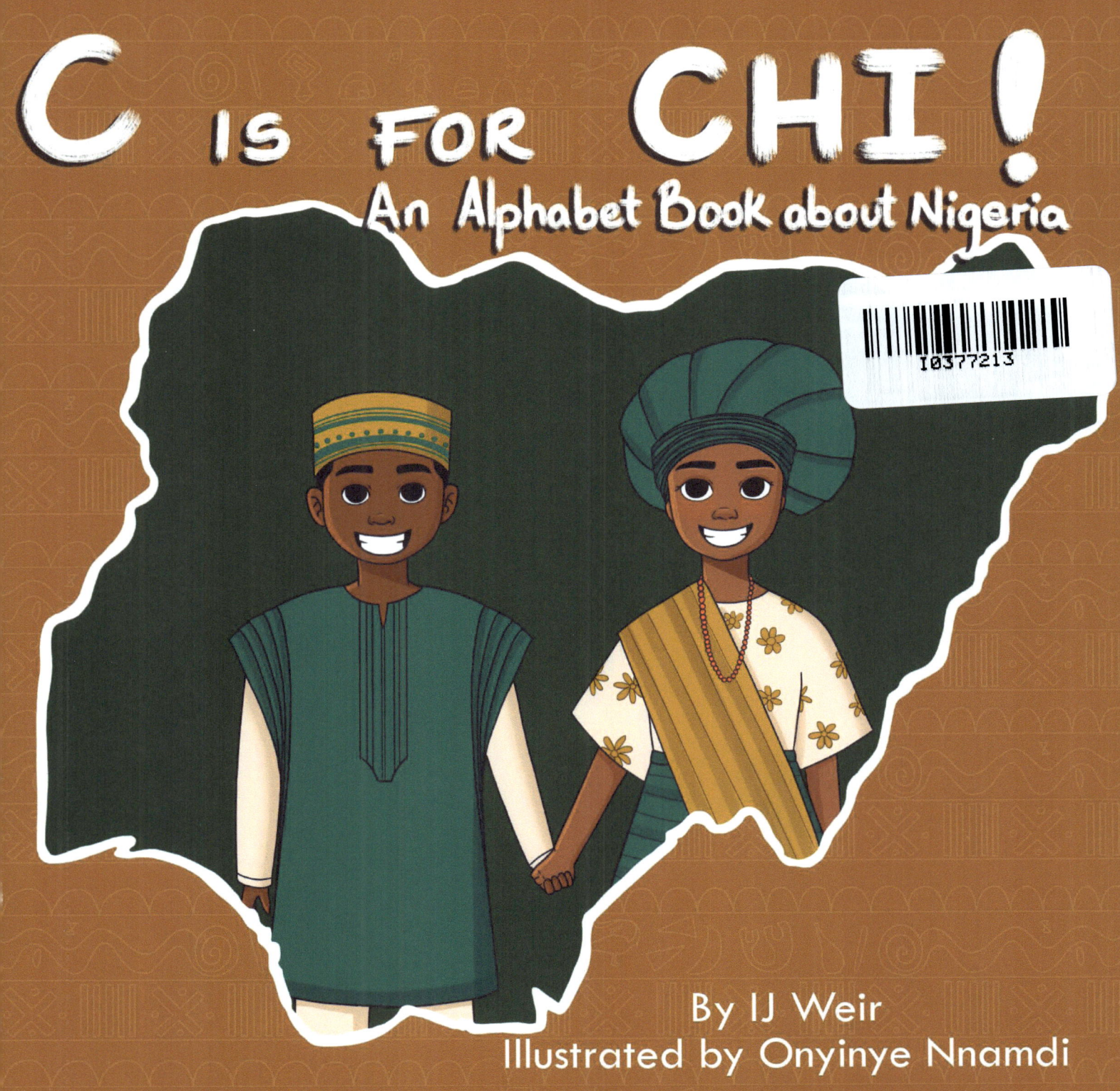

A is for Aso

Aso means victorious to the local people.
Aso rock is the largest and highest rock in
Nigeria's capital, Abuja.
You can see the whole city from the top!

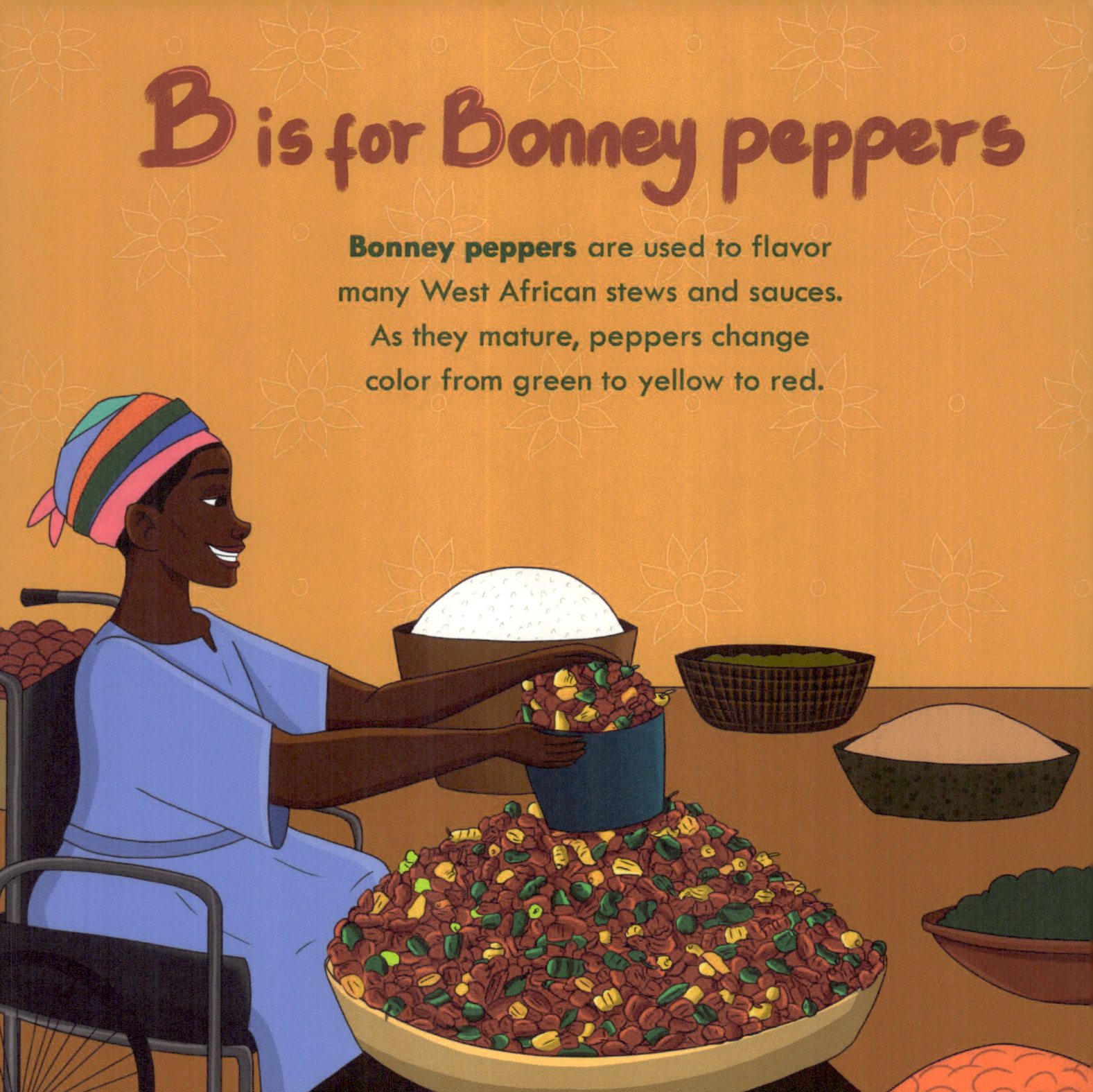

C is for Chi

The Igbo people believe each person is born with a spiritual being, or **chi**. The Ikenga is a sculpture said to represent a person's **chi**, power, and strength.

D is for Dundun

Dundun drums are a very important part of Nigerian culture. Long ago, griots, or storytellers, sent messages to other villages using the Dundun, or 'talking drum'.

E is for Egusi

Egusi are seeds from plants like squash or melon. Egusi soup is a popular dish made with Egusi, leafy vegetables, and seasonings.

F is for Football

The Nigerian national **football** team plays all around the world. In Nigeria, the team plays in Abuja, the capital city.
Do you play football?

G is for Gèlè

In Nigeria, a cloth head scarf is called **gèlè**. The Yoruba make their **gèlè** with a special hand-woven cloth called Aso oke.

H is for Hausa

Over 500 languages are spoken in Nigeria. **Hausa**, Yoruba, Igbo, Fula, and English are the most widely spoken languages across the country.

I is for Ijele

Ijele is a special masquerade featured in some Igbo ceremonies. The design takes hundreds of people many months to complete.

J is for Jollof

Families prepare **Jollof** rice for meals. The main ingredients are rice, vegetables, garlic, ginger, and meat. Yum!

K is for Kainji

Kainji National Park is the first national park in Nigeria. The park has so much wildlife. Which animals do you see?

KAINJI LAKE NATIONAL PARK

M is for Moimoi

Moimoi is a delicious savory pudding made with beans, onions, and red peppers. Many Nigerians eat moimoi with bread, sauces, or jollof rice.

O is for Osun

The **Osun** Festival is a celebration in honor of Osun, a Yoruba goddess. The festival is filled with drumming, dancing, and celebration as thousands begin the mile-long walk from the city to the river.

P is for Pidgin

"How far?!"

"Abeg!"

"Wetin?"

Pidgin is a widely spoken language throughout Nigeria. The language is a combination of words and phrases from many Nigerian languages, Portuguese, and English.

"Abi?"

"I wan chop"

"No Wahala"

Q is for Queen

Amina, Hausa warrior queen, created many trade routes throughout Northern Africa. She is honored as a statue in Lagos.

R is for Rafia

Dried **raffia** palm fronds are tied together to make a cooking utensil called the Ijabe. The tool mashes or blends vegetables inside pots while cooking!

S is for Swallow

Swallows are balls of yam or wheat flour.
Swallows are traditionally served with stew, soup, or sauces.
Would you try swallows?

T is for Talatin da uku

Talatin da uku is Hausa for the number 33. The Nigerian alphabet has 33 letters.

Every Nigerian language can be written using these letters!

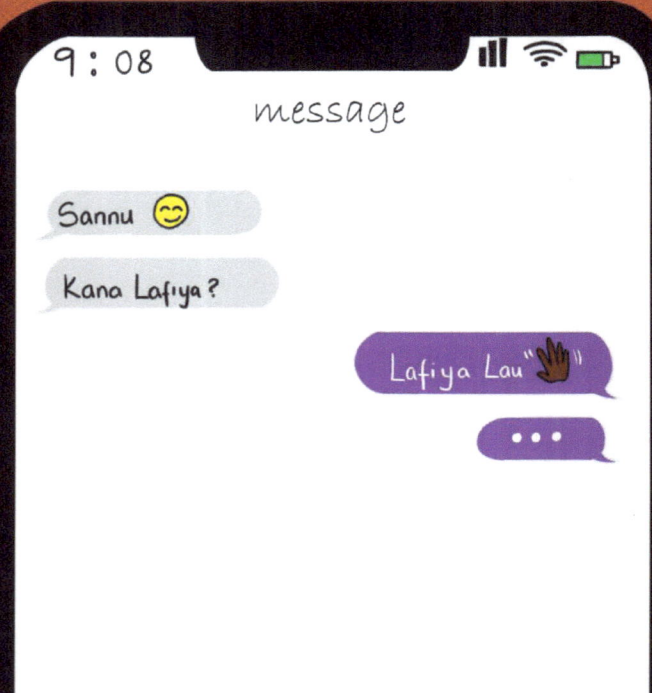

V is for Victoria Island

Victoria Island is a neighborhood in Lagos that is home to both locals and visitors. The island is a popular destination for shopping, entertainment, and restaurants!

W is for Wara

Wara, also known as Nigerian cheese curds, can be served as a fried snack or with a meal.

X is Ko si tẹlẹ

Nigerian languages do not have the letter 'X' in the alphabet. It is **ko si tẹlẹ** - it does not exist!

Y is for Yam

The Igbo people consider the **yam** as the king of all crops. The New Yam Festival celebrates the time of harvest and the beginning of a new planting season.

Z is for Zobo

Zobo is a Nigerian beverage made from the hibiscus plant. Some have zobo with ice, while others add cucumber and citrus to the drink. Would you try some refreshing zobo? Cheers!

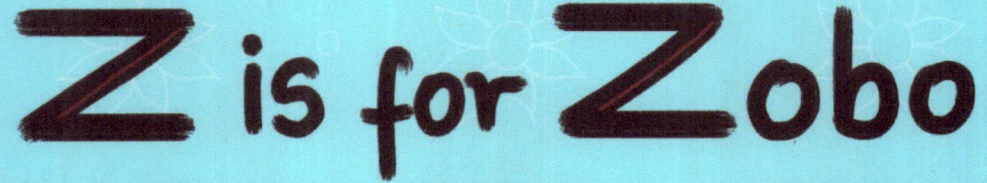

To Naomi

C is for Chi! An Alphabet Book About Nigeria

Copyright © 2021 by IJ Weir

All Rights Reserved. No part of this publication may be reproduced, stored in a retrieval system or transmitted, in any form or by any means— electronic, mechanical, photocopying, recording or otherwise— without prior written permission from the publisher, except for the inclusion of brief quotations in a review.

The resources in this book are provided for informational purposes only.

Printed in United States of America

For information about this title or to order other books and/or electronic media, contact the publisher:

Vessel and Spice LLC

4445 Corporation Ln., STE 264

Virginia Beach, VA 23462

ISBN: 978-1-7368004-0-9 (e-book)

ISBN: 978-1-7368004-1-6 (paperback)

ISBN: 978-1-7368004-2-3 (hardcover)

www.ingramcontent.com/pod-product-compliance
Lightning Source LLC
Chambersburg PA
CBHW042256100526
44589CB00002B/35